From Brokenness to Community

From Brokenness
to Community

JEAN VANIER

The Wit Lectures
Harvard University
The Divinity School

PAULIST PRESS
New York and Mahwah, N.J.

Library of Congress Cataloging-in Publication Data

Vanier, Jean, 1928–
    From brokenness to community/Jean Vanier.
        p.   cm.—(The Wit lectures)
    ISBN 0-8091-3341-5 (paper)
    1. Church work with the mentally handicapped.
2. Christian communities—Catholic Church.   3. Church
work with the poor—Catholic Church.   4. Catholic
Church—Membership.   5. Spiritual life—Catholic
Church.   6. Catholic Church—Charities.   7. Vanier,
Jean, 1928–   .   8. Arche
(Association)   I. Title.   II. Series.
BX2347.8.M4V25   1992
259'.4—dc20   92-4796
                                                  CIP

Published by Paulist Press
997 Macarthur Blvd.
Mahwah, N.J. 07430

Printed and bound in the United States of America

FOREWORD

*I*t is a real joy for me to introduce these Harvard lectures by Jean Vanier, especially since Harvard University and Jean Vanier have had a great impact on my life.

I will never forget the morning when Jean Vanier taught in my course at the Harvard Divinity School. The class was to start at 8:30 a.m. and I was afraid he wouldn't make it on time, considering the heavy Cambridge morning traffic. Elizabeth Buckley, who was driving him, knew the back streets of Cambridge and managed to bring him to Andover Hall one minute before the class was supposed to start. As always, he radiated calm and peace, while I was all nerves. As he walked into the building, with his slightly stooped form, his strong features and his white, unkempt hair, and wearing his seemingly permanent blue corduroy pants and patched-up windbreaker jacket, he greeted me with a big smile and handed me a small mosaic of the Virgin and Child made by the handicapped members of the L'Arche Community in France.

It was that tall, self-confident, poorly dressed,

but aristocratic-looking man who had made me wonder whether Harvard was the best place for me. I loved teaching there. I was excited about the great variety of students and felt challenged by the questions they, especially the women students, were raising. But Harvard didn't feel like home for me. Somehow I knew that I was looking for something that could nurture my heart in a more basic way and offer me a better context for my spiritual growth. When I met Jean Vanier for the first time, I immediately sensed that he not only understood the desire of my soul, but also knew how to respond to it. He invited me to come to his community and discover the treasure of the poor. It wasn't immediately clear to me that I should leave Harvard and join L'Arche, but, on knowing Jean, a search was set in motion that finally led me to leave the academic world and join the life with mentally handicapped people. It was during my time of soul-searching that Jean Vanier came to the Harvard Divinity School to speak in my course on Christian spirituality.

I no longer know exactly what he said, but much of what he said radiated the same spirit as the Harvard lectures published in this book. It is a spirit of simplicity, a spirit of gratitude, a spirit of celebration, fed by a deep love for the poor. Jean always tells stories, just as Jesus did. He speaks about the handicapped people he lives with or visits in one of the many L'Arche communities throughout the world. And these people are his teachers. He often says, "I am being taught in the University of the poor."

After Jean's first visit to Harvard Divinity School, people spoke for a long time about the experience of being in his presence. His many simple stories and the reverence and joy with which he told them had been a radical challenge to all there. Underneath all his simple and seemingly unthreatening words, the question lay hidden: "To whom are you called?" Jean Vanier's disarming but spiritually demanding presence did not allow his listeners or readers to remain neutral. This is also the power of this text.

Today, seven years after Jean Vanier came to "teach" at the Harvard Divinity School, I have become the pastor of the L'Arche-Daybreak Community, and Jean has continued to visit the different L'Arche communities in the world and call people to radical discipleship wherever he is invited. On one of his visits to the United States of America, he returned to Harvard and presented these lectures. I am very glad that they are now made available in this book. They witness to the importance of the meeting between the University of the learned and the University of the poor. I trust that in this meeting an ever deeper understanding of true discipleship will emerge.

Henri J. M. Nouwen

INTRODUCTION

*I*n November 1988, Jean Vanier delivered two lectures at Harvard Divinity School and inaugurated the Harold M. Wit Lecture Series on Living a Spiritual Life in the Contemporary Age.

The series was established by a generous gift from two Harvard College alumni, Harold Wit, Class of 1949, and Arthur Dubow, Class of 1954. Its purpose has been eloquently stated by Mr. Wit in his letter instituting the lectureship:

What I thought might be a gift to young people at Harvard and to others open to such possibilities would be to bring to the Harvard community in a series of lectures unusual individuals who radiate in their thought, word, and being those spiritual qualities and values that have been so inspiring and encouraging to me along my path. This in the hope that those listening to the lectures and being privileged to be in the good company of such persons might likewise be inspired and encouraged.

As we inaugurate the publication of this initial volume of lectures, I want to thank Harold Wit and Arthur Dubow for this significant new lecture series and for their insight and wisdom in seeing the importance of this effort.

We were honored to have as our inaugural lecturer Jean Vanier, founder of the international L'Arche movement. Mr. Vanier is a leading interpreter of the contemporary spiritual life. Born in 1928, a son of the late nineteenth governor-general of Canada, he was educated in England and Canada and served as a naval officer in both countries. He received his doctorate in moral philosophy in Paris, and taught philosophy in Toronto. In 1964 he invited two men with mental disabilities to move into a small house with him in Trosly-Breuil, France. The community that grew from that household came to be called L'Arche, or "The Ark." Since that time ninety-five such communities, devoted to recognizing and nurturing the dignity of the disabled, have sprung up in twenty-four countries worldwide.

L'Arche communities seek to create for people with mental disabilities a family-like environment in which they gain a deeper sense of their own worth through the bond of friendship. In addition to L'Arche, the Faith and Light associations which regularly bring together people with a handicap, their families and friends in prayer and celebration, and the Faith and Sharing retreat movement, both testify mightily to Jean Vanier's understanding that the most precious human gifts are rooted in weakness, and that in welcoming the poorest and most vulnerable among us, it is we who will be spiritually nourished by them. As Mr. Vanier has written, "If we choose to come to L'Arche, it is in order to enter into a relationship with people who have a mental handicap, and through this relationship of friendship help them to discover the light and the hidden beauty which lies in their weakness . . . what characterizes assistants who come to L'Arche is that they accept to share their lives with devalued people, to establish real bonds with them. This choice goes against the current values of society which call, rather, for 'going up' the social scale. Climbing the ladder of a certain hierarchy. From this point of view L'Arche goes against our culture."

The communities of L'Arche are grounded "on welcome of the poor and on religious faith." They are anchored in a spiritual discipline focused on the life of prayer. The identity of the L'Arche movement is, again in Mr. Vanier's words, "founded on love for people with mental disabilities. If we keep our eyes fixed on them, if we are faithful to them, we will always find our path. We are constantly called to draw this love from the heart of God, and from God's mysterious presence at the heart of poor people."

Jean Vanier filled two large, crowded lecture halls at Harvard with his quiet tones and searching, powerful message. His witness of faith in an academic setting was an extraordinary experience for all who attended, and it is our hope that these published lectures will convey to an even wider audience his deeply moving spiritual message about love for the poor and weak, and about the human heart as the dwelling place of God.

These lectures and their insights are indeed the fruits of what has engaged Jean Vanier for many years—prayer, study, reflection, and life lived both in "the wisdom of community" and in a covenant of love and faithfulness with those who are weak. As you read the lectures, I think you will agree that there can be no more timely message for us than the one Jean Vanier brings.

Ronald F. Thiemann
Dean and John Lord O'Brian Professor of Divinity
Harvard Divinity School
Cambridge, Massachusetts

1

THROUGH THEIR WOUNDS
WE ARE HEALED

*I*n some ways it seems very strange, even absurd that I should be with you all here today in Harvard. I've come to you from L'Arche, where I have been living for the last twenty-six years with men and women who have mental disabilities. Just yesterday I was with my community in Trosly: a beautiful community made up of many very simple people, all of them quite limited in their capacities. Most of them can neither read nor write; they move slowly or clumsily. Some cannot even speak or walk or eat on their own.

And I come here to tell you how much life these people have given me, that they have an incredible gift to bring to our world, that they are a source of hope, peace and perhaps salvation for our wounded world, and that if we are open to them, if we welcome them, they give us life and lead us to Jesus and the good news.

Yes, it seems quite absurd for me to be saying this to you, at Harvard, where people are certainly not limited in their intellectual capacities!

Yet, it is my belief that in our mad world

where there is so much pain, rivalry, hatred, violence, inequality, and oppression, it is people who are weak, rejected, marginalized, counted as useless, who can become a source of life and of salvation for us as individuals as well as for our world. And it is my hope that each one of you may experience the incredible gift of the friendship of people who are poor and weak, that you too, may receive life from them. For they call us to love, to communion, to compassion and to community.

I am always very moved as I read the gospel, the "good news," and see how Jesus lives and acts, how he enters into relationship with each person: "Will you come with me? I love you. Will you enter into communion with me?" He calls each one he meets into a personal, intimate relationship with himself. But as he invites people to follow him, he is also telling them that they must make a choice. If they choose one thing, it means refusing another. If they choose to follow Jesus, they receive a gift of love and communion, but at the same time they must say "no" to the ways of the world and accept loss; they must own their choice.

Then Jesus calls his friends into community with others who have been chosen for the same path. This is when all the problems begin! We see the disciples squabbling among themselves, wondering who is the greatest, the most important among them! Community is a wonderful place, it is life-giving; but it is also a place of pain because it is a place of truth and of growth—the revelation of our pride, our fear, and our brokenness.

Then Jesus says to his followers: "Now go! Go out to the world and bring the good news to others; do not keep it for yourselves. Heal, liberate and bring life and hope to others, especially to the poor, the weak, the blind and the lame."

I was thirteen when I joined the British navy during World War II. My adolescent years were taken up in the world of efficiency, controlling and commanding others. I was a technician of destruction. My last ship was the Canadian aircraft carrier, "The Magnificent." However, after a few years, I felt called by Jesus to take another path, the path of peace. I left the navy and did a doctorate in philosophy in Paris. I started teaching philosophy at the University of Toronto. Then, through a priest-friend, I had the good fortune of meeting people with mental disabilities.

In 1964 I took from an asylum two men, Raphael and Philip, and we began to live together. I did not know I was founding the first of many L'Arche communities. I simply felt called to live with these two men who had suffered rejection and a lot of inner pain and perhaps with a few others like them. When I had begun living with them, I soon started to discover the immense pain in their hearts. When we talk of the poor, or of announcing the good news to the poor, we should never idealize the poor. Poor people are hurt; they are in pain. They can be very angry, in revolt or in depression.

I have had the occasion to visit quite a number of asylums and psychiatric hospitals in France and in other countries. It can be very painful to go into certain hospitals, to see men and women crying out for love, roaming around with nothing to do, hitting their heads on the floor, living in a world of dream and of psychosis. Some places smell of urine or of disinfectant. If you have had the privilege of penetrating into some of these places, you will have seen unbearable pain. It is difficult to be present there.

Many people in our modern world are living in unbearable situations. I was told that just a few weeks ago a new place was opened in Boston for homeless people. The day it opened, four hundred people were there; there are some four thousand homeless people in Boston. Every evening they line up in order to be admitted for the night at the armory building. The next morning, after a cup of coffee, they are put back onto the streets. Then they roam around all day until the next evening. Many of them have been discharged from psychiatric hospitals or big institutions and have nowhere else to go. There is much anger, deep depression and intense pain inside them. When such pain becomes too much, then people tend to slip into a world of dream. Reality is just too painful.

The world of dream or of psychosis can in some way be easier to bear.

Our L'Arche communities are also places of pain because they are founded on people who have been through a great deal of anguish. Today, in richer countries, hospitals and asylums may be cleaner, but the same men and women are still there crying out for a home and for love. Big institutions cannot be a home. Sometimes people have been put in residences, but frequently these residences are not a home either, and they are not well accepted by neighbors.

For twenty-five years now I have had the privilege of living with men and women with disabilities. I have discovered that even though a person may have severe brain damage, that is not the source of his or her greatest pain. The greatest pain is rejection, the feeling that nobody really wants you "like that." The feeling that you are seen as ugly, dirty, a burden, of no value. That is the pain I have discovered in the hearts of our people.

When I talk to people about Eric, who was blind, deaf and had severe brain damage, I am often asked what he understands or if he can even experience suffering. Perhaps some of you would ask the same question. And yet we all know that a child, even on the day of his or her birth, knows whether he or she is loved. And if the child feels loved, the body is relaxed, the eyes are bright, there is a smile on the face; in some way the flesh becomes "transparent." A child that is loved is beautiful.

But what happens when children feel they are not loved? There is tension, fear, loneliness and terrible anguish, which we can call "inner pain," the opposite of "inner peace." Children are too small and weak to be able to fend for themselves; they have no defense mechanisms. If a child feels unloved and unwanted, he or she will develop a broken self-image. I have never heard any of the men or women whom we have welcomed into our community criticize their parents, even though many of them have suffered a great deal from rejection or abandonment in their families. Rather than blaming their parents, they blame themselves. "If I am not loved, it is because I am not lovable, I am no good. I am evil."

Of course, it is not only people with mental disabilities who are wounded and suffering from this broken self-image. Many people in our world today are living deep inner pain and anguish because as children they were not valued, welcomed, loved. I personally discovered this terrible pain living with our people in L'Arche.

Another moving discovery I made when I began to live with Raphael and Philip was of their deep cry for communion. This was a cry for love and friendship; it flowed from their loneliness and inner pain. You have surely experienced that too if you have visited people in institutions. Suddenly

14

you are surrounded by men and women saying to you (at least through the look in their eyes): "Will you be my friend? Am I important to you? Do I have any value?" Some of these people may seem to be hiding away in a corner of the room, hiding behind the bars of self-hatred or in a world of dream and psychosis. Still others might be hitting their heads on the wall. But in each one there is that same cry for love, friendship and communion. At the same time, in many of them there is also the deep fear that nobody can really love them, that nobody really wants them, because they are "dirty," "evil," "no good."

My experience has shown that when we welcome people from this world of anguish, brokenness and depression, and when they gradually discover that they are wanted and loved as they are and that they have a place, then we witness a real transformation—I would even say "resurrection." Their tense, angry, fearful, depressed body gradually becomes relaxed, peaceful and trusting. This shows through the expression on the face and through all their flesh. As they discover a sense of belonging, that they are part of a "family," then the will to live begins to emerge. I do not believe it is of any value to push people into doing things unless this desire to live and to grow has begun to emerge.

Living with men and women with mental disabilities has helped me to discover what it means to live in communion with someone. To be in communion means to *be with* someone and to discover that we actually belong together. Communion means accepting people just as they are, with all their limits and inner pain, but also with their gifts and their beauty and their capacity to grow: to see the beauty inside of all the pain. To love someone is not first of all to do things *for* them, but to reveal to them their beauty and value, to say to them through our attitude: "You are beautiful. You are important. I trust you. You can trust yourself." We all know well that we can do things for others and in the process crush them, making them feel that they are incapable of doing things by themselves. To love someone is to reveal to them their capacities for life, the light that is shining in them.

To be in communion with someone also means to *walk with* them. Those of you who have had the privilege of accompanying people in distress and inner pain know that it is not easy to walk with them, without having any answers to their problems or solutions for their pain. For many people in pain there is no solution; for a mother who has just lost her child or for a woman who has just been abandoned by her husband, there is no answer, there is just the pain. What they need is a friend willing to walk with them in all that pain. They do not need someone to tell them to try to forget the pain, because they won't. It is too deep. When a child has experienced rejection, you can say all sorts of nice things to the child, but that will not take away the pain. It will take a long time for that pain to diminish and it will probably never completely disappear.

Some of the men and women I have been living with for a number of years now are still in quite deep anguish. They are more peaceful than they were, but there are still moments when anguish surges up in them. The essential at such moments is to walk with them, accepting them just as they are, to allow them to be themselves. It is important for them to know that they can be themselves, that even though there are wounds, and pain in them, they are loved. It is a liberating experience for them to realize they do not have to conform to any preconceived idea about how they *should* be.

But this communion is not fusion. Fusion leads to *confusion*. In a relationship of communion, you are you and I am I; I have my identity and you have yours. I must be myself and you must be yourself. We are called to grow together, each one becoming more fully himself or herself. Communion, in fact, gives the freedom to grow. It is not possessiveness. It entails a deep listening to others, helping them to become more fully themselves.

When Jane came to us from the psychiatric hospital, she was full of anger and inner pain. She used to hit her head with her fist. Over the ten years she has been with us, she has grown more peaceful. Her eyes are now bright with life. She still cannot speak or walk, but it is as if her flesh has in some way been transformed.

When I was in the navy, I was taught to give orders to others. That came quite naturally to me! All my life I had been taught to climb the ladder, to seek promotion, to compete, to be the best, to win prizes. This is what society teaches us. In doing so, we lose community and communion. It was not natural or easy for me to live in communion with people, just to be with them. How much more difficult it was for me to be in communion with people who could hardly speak or had little to speak about.

Communion did not come easily to me. I had to change and to change quite radically. When you have been taught from an early age to be first, to win, and then suddenly you sense that you are being called by Jesus to go down the ladder and to share your life with those who have little culture, who are poor and marginalized, a real struggle breaks out within oneself. As I began living with people like Raphael and Philip, I began to see all the hardness of my heart. It is painful to discover the hardness in one's own heart. Raphael and the others were crying out simply for friendship and I did not quite know how to respond because of the other forces within me, pulling me to go up the ladder. But over the years, the people I live with in L'Arche have been teaching and healing me.

They have been teaching me that behind the

need for me to win, there are my own fears and anguish, the fear of being devalued or pushed aside, the fear of opening up my heart and of being vulnerable or of feeling helpless in front of others in pain; there is the pain and brokenness of my own heart.

I discovered something which I had never confronted before, that there were immense forces of darkness and hatred within my own heart. At particular moments of fatigue or stress, I saw forces of hate rising up inside me, and the capacity to hurt someone who was weak and was provoking me! That, I think, was what caused me the most pain: to discover who I really am, and to realize that maybe I did not want to know who I really was! I did not want to admit all the garbage inside me. And then I had to decide whether I would just continue to pretend that I was okay and throw myself into hyperactivity, projects where I could forget all the garbage and prove to others how good I was. Elitism is the sickness of us all. We all want to be on the winning team. That is at the heart of apartheid and every form of racism. The important thing is to become conscious of those forces in us and to work at being liberated from them and to discover that the worst enemy is inside our own hearts not outside!

It took time for me to discover that Marie-Jo's cry for communion was revealing my own poverty and my own wounds. Once you have realized that, either you run away or else you have to come to terms with it, with the help of brothers and sisters in community and with the help of God. The love and support of community gives you the certitude you are loved just as you are, with all your wounds, and that you can grow through all that. People may come to our communities because they want to serve the poor; they will only stay once they have discovered that they themselves are the poor.

And then they discover something extraordinary: that Jesus came to bring the good news to *the poor*, not to those who *serve* the poor! I think we can only truly experience the presence of God, meet Jesus, receive the good news, in and through our own poverty, because the kingdom of God belongs to the poor, the poor in spirit, the poor who are crying out for love.

It seems clear to me today that if someone is called to live with wounded people, with mental disabilities or with mental illness, people with drug problems, or whatever the wounds may be, he or she has to discover the presence of God there —that God is present in the poverty and wounds of their hearts. God is not just present in their capacity to heal but rather in their need to be healed. We can only truly love people who are different, we can only discover that difference is a treasure and not a threat, if in some way our hearts are becoming enfolded in the heart of the Father, if somewhere God is putting into our broken hearts that love that is in God's own heart for each and every human being. For God is truly in love with people, and with every individual human being.

I do not believe we can truly enter into our own inner pain and wounds and open our hearts to others unless we have had an experience of God, unless we have been touched by God. We must be touched by the Father in order to experience, as the prodigal son did, that no matter how wounded we may be, we are loved. And not only are we loved, but we too are called to heal and to liberate. This healing power in us will not come from our capacities and our riches, but in and through our poverty. We are called to discover that God can bring peace, compassion and love through *our* wounds.

The cry for communion in the poor and the broken makes us touch our own inner pain. We discover our own brokenness and the barriers inside of us, which have gradually been formed during our childhood to save us from inner pain. These barriers prevent us from being present to others, in communion with others; they incite us to compete and to dominate others. It is when we have realized this that we cry out to God. And then we meet the "Paraclete" whom Jesus and the Father have promised to send to us. The word "paracleta" means "the one who answers the cry." It is not possible to receive the Spirit unless we cry out, and unless that cry surges up from the consciousness of our own wound, our pain, and our brokenness.

I am deeply moved as I witness the growth toward wholeness and the holiness of the people with disabilities with whom I live. Some of us have been living together now for twenty years and more. They are men and women of real maturity. When young people come to help in L'Arche, we find they are much less mature. We see a discrepancy in the maturity between those who have a handicap and those who have come to help. So many young people coming to L'Arche today do not know how to make choices or have too many choices; often they are not sure of the meaning of their lives; they themselves are deeply broken.

As I live with Marie, Jane, Didier and all the others, I understand why Jesus trembled in the Spirit and said: "Blessed are you, Father, Lord of heaven and earth, for having hidden these things from the wise and the clever and revealed them to little ones," or why Paul could say: "God has chosen what is foolish in the world in order to confound the wise; God has chosen what is weak in order to confound the strong; God has chosen what is low and what is most despised."

Our people are close to God, and yet they are so little and so poor. They have known rejection and have suffered a great deal. I am always moved as I hear them speak of Jesus. When somebody asked one of our men, Peter, if he liked to pray, he said that he did. So the person continued and asked him what he did when he prayed. He replied: "I listen." Then the person asked what God says to him. Peter, a man with Down's Syndrome, looked up and said: "He just says, 'You are my beloved son.'"

When someone has lived most of his or her life in the last place and then discovers that Jesus is there in the last place as well, it is truly good news. However, when someone has always been looking for the first place and learns that Jesus is in the last place, it is confusing! Our people have their doubts, temptations and inner struggles, of course, but in their poverty their whole being cries out to God. The beatitudes are in some way closer to their reality. There is a holiness and a wholeness in them. In all their littleness and poverty, God is close. I am touched by another man in my house who is quite poor and fragile: Didier. I still have difficulty understanding him when he speaks. One time, however, our whole house went to a monastery for a weekend. On the last evening, I asked everyone what had touched them most. Didier said, "When Father Gilbert was speaking, my heart was burning."

Yes, the broken and the oppressed have taught me a great deal and have changed me quite radically. They have helped me discover that healing takes place at the bottom of the ladder, not at the top. Their cry for communion has taught me something about my own humanity, my own brokenness—that we are all wounded, we are all poor. But we are all the people of God; we are all loved and are being guided. They have taught me what it means to be with brothers and sisters in communion, in community. They have revealed to me the well of tenderness that is hidden in my own heart and which can give life to others.

The broken and oppressed are teaching me what the good news is really about.

One of the most moving moments for me in the gospel is the meeting of Jesus with the woman from Samaria. The Samaritans were a very rejected people. The Jews despised them. And this Samaritan woman was rejected and marginalized by her own people as well, for she had lived with five men; she was not living according to the laws of God. This woman is perhaps one of the poorest, most broken women of the gospels.

When Jesus meets her, he does not tell her to get her act together. Rather, he exposes to her his own need. He says to her: "Give me to drink." It is good to see how Jesus approaches broken people —not from a superior position but from a humbler, lower position even from his fatigue: "I need you." In fact Jesus seems to be more "at home" with the leper, the publican, the poor and the weak, the children, than with the Pharisee and the rich and the wise. So you can understand a bit better what a gift it is for me to live in community with Didier, Raphael, Marie-Jo, and each one in L'Arche.

However, there is still a paradox. Those with whom Jesus identifies himself are regarded by society as misfits. And yet Jesus *is* that person who is hungry; Jesus *is* that woman who is confused and naked. As I carried in my arms Eric who was blind, deaf and with severe brain damage, I sensed that paradox: "Whosoever welcomes one of these little ones in my name, welcomes me; and whoever welcomes me, welcomes the one who sent me."

Wouldn't it be extraordinary if that were true? Wouldn't it be extraordinary if we all discovered that? The face of the world would be changed. We would then no longer want to compete in going up the ladder to meet God in the light, in the sun and in beauty, to be honored because of our theological knowledge. Or if we did want knowledge it would be because we believe that our knowledge and theology are important only so long as they are used to serve and honor the poor.

2

COMMUNITY: A PLACE OF
BONDING, CARING AND MISSION

*D*uring the synod concerned with the vocation and the role of the laity in the Roman Catholic Church, which took place in Rome in 1987, the Faith and Light communities of Rome invited all the bishops to come to a gathering of their communities, made up of people with intellectual disabilities, their parents and their many friends, especially young people. Only a few bishops came. The community of L'Arche in Rome came also, with Armando, an amazing eight year old boy they had welcomed.

Armando cannot walk or talk and is very small for his age. He came to us from an orphanage where he had been abandoned. He no longer wanted to eat because he no longer wanted to live cast off from his mother. He was desperately thin and was dying of lack of food. After a while in our community where he found people who held him, loved him, and wanted him to live, he gradually began to eat again and to develop in a remarkable way. He still cannot walk or talk or eat by himself, his body is twisted and broken, and he has a se-

26

vere mental disability, but when you pick him up, his eyes and his whole body quiver with joy and excitement and say: "I love you." He has a deep therapeutic influence on people.

I asked one of the bishops if he wanted to hold Armando in his arms. He did. I watched the two of them together as Armando settled into his arms and started to quiver and smile, his little eyes shining. A half hour later I came to see if the bishop wanted me to take back Armando. "No, no," he replied. I could see that Armando in all his littleness, but with all the power of love in his heart, was touching and changing the heart of that bishop. Bishops are busy men, they have power and they frequently suffer acts of aggression, so they have to create solid defense mechanisms. But someone like Armando can penetrate the barriers they—and all of us—create around our hearts; Armando can awaken us to love and call forth the well of living waters and of tenderness hidden inside of us. Armando is not threatening. He does not awaken our sexuality. He just says "I love you; I love being with you."

Many people know they have a head because they have learned that two and two are four. They know that they have hands because they can cook eggs and do other things. Many know they have a sexuality because they have experienced strong emotions. But what they do not always know is that they have a well deep inside of them. If that well is tapped, springs of life and of tenderness flow forth. It has to be revealed to each person that these waters are there and that they can rise up from each one of us and flow over people, giving them life and a new hope.

That is the power of Armando. In some mysterious way, in all his brokenness, he reveals to us our own brokenness, our difficulties in loving, our barriers and hardness of heart. If he is so broken and so hurt and yet is still such a source of life, then I too am allowed to look at my own brokenness and to trust that I too can give life to others. I do not have to pretend that I am better than others and that I have to win in all the competitions. It's O.K. to be myself, just as I am, in my uniqueness. That, of course, is a very healing and liberating experience. I am allowed to be myself, with all my psychological and physical wounds, with all my limitations but with all my gifts too. And I can trust that I am loved just as I am, and that I too can love and grow.

The other thing people with disabilities have revealed to me is their incredible capacity for creating community and bringing people together. Experience has shown that one person, all alone, can never heal another. A one-to-one situation is not a good situation. It is important to bring broken people into a community of love, a place where they feel accepted and recognized in their gifts, and have a sense of belonging. That is what wounded people need and want most.

Today I want to talk to you about *belonging* and about *community.* As followers of Jesus, we are called to look at Jesus and see how he lived and moved among people. First of all he called people into a deep relationship of communion with himself. He looked at them, loved them, and said: "Will you come and be with me? Will you enter into a friendship with me?" And then he would say: "If you want to enter into that relationship, if you accept my love, you must own your choice, and accept loss. If you follow me, then you will have to lose something. You have to lose some material goods and attachments you have." That is the first thing: it is a relationship which implies choice—really choosing, following a call, and accepting loss which will imply grieving and pain.

Then Jesus calls those who accept this communion of love with him into community, to live and be with others who also have been called. This is where even deeper grief begins. I love to see how human and like us the first disciples of Jesus were. As soon as his back is turned they start to fight among themselves: "Who is the most important, who is the best?" Community is the place where are revealed all the darkness and anger, jealousies and rivalry hidden in our hearts.

Community is a place of pain, because it is a

place of loss, a place of conflict, and a place of death. But it is also a place of resurrection.

Finally as soon as the community of the disciples is born, Jesus sends them: "Go. Go and announce the good news to the poor, but go with nothing—not even two pairs of sandals. Don't take two tunics, don't take any money, don't take any food. Go with nothing. Go poorly and do the impossible."

What is the "impossible"? It is liberation. To liberate people from the demons of fear, of loneliness, of hatred and of egoism that shackle them. To liberate people so that they also can love, heal, and liberate others. But in order to do that, you must go in poverty and experience the life of God flowing within your own flesh. You will give life but a life that flows from the heart of God. You will bring people to new life, a new hope. The mystery of community lies between the call of Jesus to communion with him, "Come and be with me," and the sending off to announce the good news of love, to give life to other people.

Community is a place of conflict: conflict inside each one of us. There is first of all the conflict between the values of the world and the values of community, between togetherness and independence. It is painful to lose one's independence, and to come into togetherness—not just proximity—to make decisions together and not all alone. Loss of independence is painful, particularly in a world where we have been told to be independent and to cultivate the feeling that "I don't need anyone else."

The next source of conflict is in learning to give space to others so that they may grow, rather than competing with them and lording over them. Our world is a world of competition. We have all been taught to live in a competitive world and to win, to be a success, and to move up the ladder of promotion and to get ahead. It is hard then in community to stand back in order to help others grow and exercise their gifts. There is then in community a loss of aggressive competition cultivated in our societies.

The third source of conflict is similar to the second. It is the conflict between caring for people and caring only for oneself. To really care for the growth and freedom of other people means to sacrifice our own freedom. It means to discover that our greatest freedom is to help others walk to freedom.

The fourth source of conflict is between being open and being closed. Maybe in the first three conflicts I mentioned we can really blame the culture of our richer countries, where people are called from an early age to win prizes, to walk to independence, to become a success. But this fourth danger can also be seen in poorer countries where the big, extended family has the appearance of community, but if you look more closely you will discover how often the extended family is closed. In a tribe, people are called to sacrifice their personal consciousness for a collective consciousness. In order to have greater security, people can sacrifice their personal growth, freedom and becoming, to the god of belonging—belonging which gives security and power. There are quite a number of pseudo-communities where there is a strong sense of belonging, but a death to personal becoming. A community which is called to keep people open is a vulnerable community that takes risks. It does not hang on to its own security and power obliging people to stay.

There is a myth about community, just as there is a myth about marriage. The myth of marriage is "they lived happily ever after." The reality of marriage is that it is a place where a man and a woman are called to sacrifice their egos on the altar of their desire to create one body. Community also means death to ego, in order that people might grow to become one body, truly belonging to each other, not in a closed way but in a mysterious way where each one is growing in inner freedom.

To accept the risk of personal consciousness and growth to inner freedom can be painful; it is never easy to follow the light inside of oneself when others do not seem to agree. Communities can tend to close in upon themselves. But belonging should always be a means to personal becoming. It is accepting the risk of dying to aggressiveness and rivalry in order to discover a new freedom and a new fecundity—a new way of giving life to others, but still to belong to others, to be in "one body" with them.

I sense very deeply in the churches and in the world today a double movement. First there is a strong movement for personal and collective independence cultivated by a desire for economic progress. The extended family in Africa and India, and in many other countries, is being deeply wounded by the desire for individual gain. In struggling to "win" at any price, members of the family lose a sense of community. More and more people are seeking the individual prize. In richer countries, this desire to win is instilled in children from an early age. I remember visiting a school in Canada where there was a big poster: "It Is a Crime Not To Excel." There was another poster of one car overtaking another which said: "Are You in the Passing Lane?" Right from an early age we cultivate this feeling that it is a crime not to be the best.

Yet at the same time I am sensing inside of the churches, as well as countries, a yearning for solidarity, a cry coming from people for togetherness and for love. For too long we've been walking on the road to independence. We're beginning to feel our loneliness. We're beginning to see that we can only live if we're together. We're beginning to see the immense dangers of separation, of apartheid. We're seeing that if we separate ourselves, and then create barriers around our group, we'll tend to become rivals.

Never before has the cry for nuclear disarmament been so loud. But it's even more important that there be disarmament inside human communities and inside of each one of our hearts. There's no point in having big disarmament meetings between countries if inside of our communities and neighborhoods we're not disarming ourselves in the world of competition and rivalry.

Perhaps for the first time in the history of humanity, there is a growing sense among many that we all belong to the same humanity, a yearning for peace and unity among all human beings, living on an earth we all love and respect. The yearning for community is profound; it is seen through books like M. Scott Peck's *The Different Drum: Community and Making Peace,* which was for some time a best seller. People are yearning to rediscover community. We have had enough of loneliness, independence and competition.

Perhaps it is too late. Maybe we do not have the inner force to live community. Perhaps we are all too broken, the inner pain is too great. But somewhere, in the heart of humanity today, there is a cry coming from our own loneliness and the injustices and pain of our world: a cry for community, for belonging, for togetherness and for love.

More and more people are becoming conscious that our God is not just a powerful Lord telling us to obey or be punished but our God is *family*. Our God is three persons in love with each other; our God is communion. And this beautiful and loving God is calling us humans into this life of love. We are not alone; we are called together to drop barriers, to become vulnerable, to become one. The greatest thirst of God is that "they may be one, perfectly one, totally one." But we have to die to all the powers of egoism in ourselves in order to be reborn for this new and deeper unity where our uniqueness and personal gifts and creativity are not crushed but enlivened and enhanced.

Community means caring: caring for people. Dietrich Bonhoeffer says: "He who loves community destroys community; he who loves the brethren builds community." A community is not an abstract ideal. We are not striving for perfect community. Community is not an ideal; it is people. It is you and I. In community we are called to love people just as they are with their wounds and their gifts, not as we would want them to be. Community means giving them space, helping them to grow. It means also receiving from them so that we too can grow. It is giving each other freedom; it is giving each other trust; it is confirming but also challenging each other. We give dignity to each other by the way we listen to each other, in a spirit of trust and of dying to oneself so that the other may live, grow and give.

I am deeply convinced of this, particularly, of course, when I see the pain of those people in L'Arche who have been rejected because of their intellectual disabilities. The source of their pain is their lack of self-confidence. When I was thirteen I asked my father if I could join the navy. That was during the war, and it meant crossing the Atlantic to join the British navy, at a time when one out of every three ships was being sunk by German submarines. My father just said to me: "Come and see me in my office." That, I thought, was bad news, because I never went into his office. On the appointed day I went to his office and sat in a huge armchair (which today I imagine would not seem quite so huge to me). My father asked me, "Why do you want to join the navy?" I forget what I said. All I remember is what he said: "I trust you. If that's what you want, that's what you must do." What he said was the greatest gift that he could ever have given me. By saying "I trust you," he was saying to me, "You can trust yourself. You can trust your own intuitions and deepest desires." If he had said, "That is childish; wait another four years and then you can do what you want," I'd have said to myself, "My intuition and desire are not good. They are childish. I can't really trust what I want, and I don't know what I want." My father then would have broken the power of desire and of trust inside of me.

We can give people the gift of their dignity. We can help others just by the way we listen to them and speak with them. We can show them by our own trust that what they have to say is important and good. Community is caring for people, but of course as soon as we start caring for people, we know that there are some people who will just drive us up the wall. Some we will really like, because they think like us. Then we risk falling into a world of mutual flattery. We are all so much in need of affection that when somebody gives it to us we want to hold onto it. Then we say to the other person, "You're wonderful! Keep at it! Keep flattering me! You know, it's nice." We're like little cats who need to be caressed. We then begin to purr.

But flattery doesn't help anyone to grow. It doesn't bring freedom but rather closes people up in themselves. We are attracted to certain people, and others put us off. We don't get on well with them. They trigger off our anguish. Perhaps they remind us of our fathers and mothers who were too authoritarian or possessive. Some people threaten us, others flatter us. Some meetings are joyful, and others are painful. When we begin talking about caring for people, then we begin to see how difficult it can be. In community we are called to care for *each* member of the community. We can choose our friends but we do not choose our brothers and sisters; they are *given* to us whether in family or in community.

We may be called into or choose a particular community, but once we are in the community, the brothers and sisters are given. Some will get on our nerves, others will attract us. But community means caring for *each one.* If we let ourselves be attracted to those who flatter us or who are like us, who share our ideas, then we won't grow. Growth will come as we come closer to people who are different from us and as we learn to welcome and listen even to those who trigger off our pain.

Every time I try to understand the gospels a little more, I am amazed by the incredible power of the message. At the heart of Jesus' message is: "Love your enemies. Do good to those who criticize you, who hate you. Pray for those who persecute and push you down." Our enemy is not somebody far off in a distant land. Our enemy is somebody close by who threatens us, who blocks us. Our enemy is inside, not outside, the community.

When I give retreats, I often ask people to identify their enemy. We all have an enemy in our family, in our community or place of work, somebody who threatens us, our ideas or our emotional life—somebody we're jealous of, somebody who blocks us. And Jesus says: "Love your enemies. Do good to those who hate you, who criticize you and speak evil of you; pray for those who persecute you." That is what is entirely new in the message of Christ. That is why the message of Christ is based on something extraordinary—a call to universal love, and the respect and love of difference. We are all frightened of difference. Yet when Jesus tells us to love our enemies, he is telling us about our common humanity.

At the heart of community, as we learn to care for our brothers and sisters, there is forgiveness. Reconciliation is at the heart of community. To grow in love means that we become men and women of forgiveness, of reconciliation. The heart of the message of Christ, its fundamental newness, is the promise of an inner strength which comes with the gift of the Spirit, the Holy Spirit, the third person of the family of God living inside of us, so that we can forgive and be forgiven. When I say that forgiveness is at the heart of community, I do not mean we have to learn to say simply, "You're a nuisance but I forgive you." It means discovering that I too am in part the cause of your being a nuisance, because I have dominated you, hurt you, brought fear up in you or because I haven't listened to you, or was not open to you. Forgiveness is not just saying, "I forgive you because you slammed the door." It's also: "I'm working on changing myself, because I have hurt you." We're all wounded people, and so consciously or unconsciously we can and do hurt each other. At the heart of a caring community is forgiveness, one to another. This is a principle of growth. We are forgiving each other because we yearn to grow and to become like Jesus.

Community, as I have said, is a place of pain, of the death of ego. In community we are sacrificing independence and the pseudo-security of being closed up. We can only live this pain if we are certain that for us being in community is our response to a call from God. If we do not have this certitude of faith then we won't be able to stay in community. I see this very much in our own communities. People will come to L'Arche attracted by the community; they like our community. They like it, and it's great—for a few days! When somebody says to me, "I find it very painful to live in this community, but I'm here because God has called me here," then I know that person has made a passage from dream to reality. They have found their place. We will only stay in community if we have gone through the passage from choosing community to knowing that we have been chosen for community. It is for us the place of purification, and of support, given to us by Jesus, that will lead us to a deeper love and liberation, a place where cleansed of our egocentric attitudes we will be able to give new life to others.

How is this call revealed to us? It is important

to understand and interpret the language of God. Language is very important; we must always try to understand what people are trying to say to us. In L'Arche when people cannot speak verbally, they will express themselves through their bodies. If they have a toothache or a stomachache, or if there is pain or a desire, they will reveal it to others through their body, through non-verbal language. We must learn this non-verbal language in order to understand them. I have discovered that as I become more open to body language, it helps me to understand better all human relationships. For even when people do speak, they use also non-verbal language. When you ask people "How are you?" and they answer "Fine, how are you?" you can tell by the look on their face whether it is true or not. Faces don't lie.

How then does God speak to us? Through the language of creation and events, but also in a very personal way to each one of us. How does God speak to me? Do I know how to decode the language of God? It is vital for a disciple of Jesus to learn how to interpret the messages of God. For this we need to be helped by someone wise in the ways of God. He or she can help us discern what that call is. Frequently a call of Jesus is revealed to us as we feel truly at home in a community and discover that the community for us is a place of growth in love and in total acceptance of the good news of Jesus. That is one of the signs that Jesus is saying to us: "Come and live with these brothers and sisters who may squabble together like the first of my disciples, but this is where I am calling you to be today. It might be difficult but it will be a place of growth in love for you. It is there that I will reveal to you my love."

I don't believe we can really put down roots in community unless there is that consciousness that God has called us to be there.

On the Thursday before Easter, "Holy Thursday," we live the eucharist together in my home in L'Arche. After the eucharist we have a very special meal, and then we live a very moving experience of littleness and forgiveness as we wash each other's feet. In that same evening we take time to "remember" our sacred history. We talk about how God has brought us together. I love to hear each one talking about where he or she was before coming to our community: "I was in a psychiatric hospital, in an institution, alone with my parents," and so on. And then there is a consciousness that now we are together. A few years ago we were dispersed; we did not know each other. Now we are together; we belong to each other.

We realize what an incredible gift God has given us, to bring us together from different lands of pain and loneliness, and to become one people. We become more conscious that we are responsible for each other. If one of us starts slipping away from what we are called to live, we will question each other. We will call each other to fidelity in prayer. We will confirm each other but also challenge each other, because we are part of one body. That is the work of God, the call of God.

I have a great love for the text of St. Paul in his first letter to the Corinthians, chapter 12, where he talks of the church as a body. There were obviously a few problems in the community at Corinth; some people were obviously saying, "I'm the one who knows and everybody must be like me." Paul tells them that a body is made up of eyes, of ears, of feet. What sort of a body would it be if everybody was an eye? That would be crazy. No, a body is made up of different parts. Each one is different. Then Paul goes on to say that those parts of the body which are the weakest and most hidden, the most indecent, are necessary to the body, and should be honored.

Community is not uniformity. There is a danger today, in our world, to want everybody to be the same, but then we lose our uniqueness. The incredible thing about us human beings is how unique each one of us is. The police know that, because of fingerprints. Each one of us, in every part of our body, is unique. There are no two people with the same fingerprints. Somebody calculated, in the realm of possibilities, how many real and potential fingerprints there could be since the creation of man and woman. I can tell you the zeros went a long, long way! But that means that I have to be seen as unique, as precious, as important, as valued. That is what a community is about —each person is seen as unique and has a gift to offer. Even the littlest and weakest person has a gift for the community, and that gift must be honored. Each one of us is very different one from the other. But all together we are like a symphony, an orchestra; all together we make up a beautiful bouquet of flowers. That means, however, that we must learn to love difference, to see it as a treasure and not as a threat. Community means the respect and love of difference. Then we discover that this body which is community is the place of communion.

I call you to reflect here upon the difference between communion and collaboration. Community is the place of communion. Kathryn Spink has written a very beautiful book about the community of Taizé in France, led by Brother Roger Schutz (*A Universal Heart: The Life and Vision of Brother Roger of Taizé*, 1986). The leader of the Taizé community is no longer called the prior, but the "servant of communion." Community leaders are not directors of a work being done together. They are the servants of communion. Some of our people with a handicap are servants of communion, too, for they are bringing people together; truly they are calling us to look each other in the eye and to recognize that we are all *one* people, and belong to *one* body; we love each other. Communion is essentially something that comes through touch and presence. It is manifested more in silence than by doing things. We are present one to another; we are together, and we feel a deep sense of having been called together to this place of communion. Collaboration certainly should find its basis in communion but frequently it does not. We can work together without really caring for each other or being bonded together in love and communion. This is what happens in a factory or in the armed services. We work together for a common goal. Communion however is bonding, caring and sharing which flows and finds its fulfillment in celebration.

We must learn to celebrate. I say *learn* to celebrate, because celebration is not just a spontaneous event. We have to discover what celebration is. Our world doesn't know much about celebration. We know quite a bit about parties, where we are artificially stimulated with alcohol to have fun. We know what movies and distractions are. But do we know what celebration is? Do we know how to celebrate our togetherness, our being one body? Do we really know how to use all that is human and divine to celebrate together?

The Jewish people know a great deal about celebration. Primitive people, people much closer to the earth, know what celebration is about. Once I was looking in a nightclub in Paris for a fellow who was lost. I had been told that he was there, so

I went into the nightclub and watched the people dancing. It was amazing; there was no togetherness. They weren't even holding each other; each one was doing his or her own thing. It seemed as if each one was jogging up and down all alone! Somehow we need to rediscover what dance and celebration are, what song is, what food and wine are about, what it means to put on special clothes for special events.

Sometimes when I go to visit people, they keep the television on during the meal. They may turn down the sound, but all through the meal there is the intrusion of the television images. It makes it difficult to meet and to share together. There is little sense of being called together by God to love and nourish each other. We need to rediscover celebration. That is what community is all about. TV can be a kind of death. Celebration is to share what and who we really are; it is to express our love for one another, our hopes, and to rejoice in being called together as parts of the same body. As we go from singing, dance and laughter into silence, there will be a sense of presence. Somewhere at the heart of celebration there is the consciousness of the presence of Christ. Christ is the one who is our cornerstone, the one who has drawn us together, and we rejoice because he is present with us.

The celebration I am talking about is "eucharist." This word means "giving thanks." Eucharist is community celebration—and I do not mean here just the eucharistic worship where the bread is transformed into the body of Christ, but also deep silence in a communion, one with another and with Christ. To truly celebrate is an act which belongs particularly to community. When I visit communities, I frequently ask, "How do you celebrate?" If they say, "We don't celebrate," then I know the community risks death. Celebration is not just going to eucharistic worship together. This maybe is the fulfillment of all celebrations. Celebration is being a eucharistic people who sing their thanks because they have been called together as one people in order to bring life to others.

I want to add here a word about the danger of *belonging*. Belonging should always be for *becoming*. If in some way belonging means death to the primacy of personal consciousness, then there is something wrong. I think there has always been the danger of community becoming a place of mediocrity. I remember a religious sister who had come to one of my retreats and lived there a deep experience of prayer; when she returned to her community, she felt eager for more prayer. Maybe, imprudently, she spent a lot of time in the chapel. One day the other sisters said to her: "Who do you think you are? A mystic? Teresa of Avila?" The greatest persecution can come from inside our communities; people who have fallen into mediocrity do not want others to rock the boat.

If someone receives a special call from Jesus and starts growing toward a greater love and compassion, to a deeper life of prayer in the community, there will come a moment when he or she begins to reveal the mediocrity of others and thus becomes dangerous. A prophet is always dangerous. Prophets were always killed in Jerusalem because they were dangerous. They make people ask questions about their own mediocrity but they are unwilling to face them and to seek change. A community can become a place of death, just as it can become a place of life. Bonding can stifle and bring death just as it can bring life. That is why Jesus is very subtle, calling people to community, but then sending them off to announce the good news. Community is also mission.

There is only the possibility of real growth in a community if people are deeply respected in their personal development. We continually need to have before us the challenge of our mission. We are not in a community just to protect ourselves. We are not even there just to protect our own little spiritual lives. We're there for the church, for people in pain. We have a message to give, and we have a message to receive. We have a mission, and if we are not a people of mission, then the community is in danger of closing up, and of dying.

Of course for Christians, the greatest becoming is entering into a deeper and more intimate relationship with Christ. It is, finally, a mystical union with God. Perhaps this is the heart of the message of every religion, but it is very much at the heart of the religion of Christ. We are called to be a people of freedom because we have received the Holy Spirit, and Jesus is our friend leading us to communion with the Father.

Thus community is not an end or a final goal in itself. It is the place where we can meet Christ and discover his love for humanity and for every person. Martin Buber said that the community is the place of the theophany. It is the place where we meet God in a very intimate relationship, where we can have that experience of being "seized by Christ." God loves us and draws us into the mystery and the love of the Trinity; there we can rest in his love. But community only keeps its meaning if it remains open to mission.

At this point I need to say a word about the difference between issues, causes, and mission. Today there are many groups of people. There are clubs, there are political parties. There are many forms and types of issue-oriented groups: against nuclear armament, against racism, against this or for that. There is a danger, in issue-oriented groups not based on community, that the enemy is seen as being the one outside of the group. The world gets divided between "the good" and "the bad." We are among the good; the others are the bad. In issue-oriented groups, the enemy is always outside. We must struggle against all those who are outside of our group, all those who are of the other party.

True community is different because of the realization that the evil is inside—not just inside the community, but inside me. I cannot think of taking the speck of dust out of my neighbor's eye unless I'm working on the log in my own. Evil is here in me. Warfare is inside my own community, and I am called to be an agent of peace there. But warfare is also in me and I am called to seek wholeness inside of myself. Healing begins here, in myself. Wholeness and unity begin inside of myself. If I am growing toward wholeness, then I'll be an agent of wholeness. If our community is an agent of wholeness, then it will be a source of life for the world around it.

To have a mission means to give life, to heal, and to liberate. It is to permit people to grow to freedom. When Jesus sends people off, he sends them to liberate and to heal others. That is the good news. And we can become people of liberation and of healing because we ourselves are walking along that road toward inner healing and inner liberation. Jesus calls his disciples to bear much fruit. "If you bear much fruit, you shall be my disciples, and bring glory to the Father." To bear fruit is to bring life to people. Not to judge, not to condemn, but to forgive. It is to remove our neighbor's burden. Remember those last words of

Christ: "Father, forgive." Essentially, a community is based on forgiveness and signs of forgiveness. It is not a group of people condemning or judging outsiders; it is not a people of violence. It is a people who trust that if their hearts are given to God, he will defend them.

Trusting people are vulnerable and can be easily crushed, as Jesus was crushed. A community which trusts in God rather than in the righteousness of its "cause" can always be crushed, but from that crushing will come resurrection. There is a hidden strength in being vulnerable, open, and non-violent, in being a people of the resurrection, knowing that we are loved and that God is guiding us, in all our fragility and littleness. We are not a people who think we are better. We are not an elite. We are people who are poor, but who have been drawn together by God and put their trust in God. That is what a kingdom community is about: a community that knows it has been called by God in all its poverty and weakness, and that God is love.

We are a eucharistic people which means that we are a people of thanksgiving, people who realize that we are prodigal sons and daughters. We are not called to judge or to condemn but to be instruments of life, to give life and to receive life. To be called together in community is an incredible gift. We discover in L'Arche that it is the poor and the weak who have called us together, and that our mission is to give life, one to another, inside of the community.

Because we've been called together, we are a people of celebration, but in our celebrations there is always a note of sadness because not all the people in our world are celebrating. Not everyone is rejoicing. Many today are being crucified in prisons and hospitals, or just downtown in the slum areas. Many people are lonely and in pain. Along with the celebration that rises from a community of thanksgiving, there is a note of pain but also a note of hope. We have been drawn together by God to be a sign of the resurrection and a sign of unity in this world where there is so much division and inner and outer death.

We feel small and weak, but we are gathered together to signify the power of God who transforms death into life. That is our hope, that God is doing the impossible: changing death to life inside of each of us, and that perhaps, through our community, each one of us can be agents in the world of this transformation of brokenness into wholeness, and of death into life.